For Tracy and Jemma, with love and thanks – MM

Text copyright © Miriam Moss 2010
Illustrations copyright © Adrienne Kennaway 2010
The right of Miriam Moss to be identified as the author and of Adrienne Kennaway to be
identified as the illustrator of this work has been asserted by them in accordance with
the Copyright, Designs and Patents Act, 1988 (United Kingdom).
Natural history consultant: Michael Scott

First published in Great Britain in 2010 and in the USA in 2011 by
Frances Lincoln Children's Books, 4 Torriano Mews,
Torriano Avenue, London NW5 2RZ
www.franceslincoln.com

A catalogue record for this book is available from the British Library.

ISBN 978-1-84507-984-0

Illustrated in watercolours

Set in TodaySB

Printed in Heshan, Guangdong, China by Leo Paper Products Ltd. in July 2010

1 3 5 7 9 8 6 4 2

This is the
MOUNTAIN

Miriam Moss

Illustrated by
Adrienne Kennaway

F

FRANCES LINCOLN
CHILDREN'S BOOKS

This is the place at the dawning of time,
in explosions of fire
a volcano was born.

Now a great mountain sleeps under African skies,
breathtaking, mysterious,
and crowned in ice.

At the foot of the mountain, on grasslands spread out,
graze vast herds of wildlife
in rain and in sun.

Giraffe nibble thorn leaves. In the shade of broad trees
baboons bicker and bark
with babies on backs.

This is the place where elephants come treading,
slow-rumbling, ears flapping,
swinging trunks to and fro.

Alert and uneasy the antelope are leaping,
as a proud pride of lions
moves closer to drink.

In the whispering grasslands Masai make their homesteads –
tall warriors, proud women,
children herding the goats.

In the foothills, Chagga women in bold and bright kangas
are tending their shambas,
of bananas and yams.

Higher up on the mountain, in green ferny forests,
bright birds feed on berries,
olive, juniper and fig.

In the tops of the trees, troupes of catapaulting colobus
swing in soft shafts of sunlight,
with streaming white tails.

Higher still on the mountain, by waterfall and small stream,
stands a shy Suni antelope,
so silent, so small.

In this place at sunset, busy bush pigs run squealing,
while bushbuck and eland
crop grasses with calm.

Mist hangs on the tree line, looking up into moorland,
where slopes of giant groundsel
stand on tall, palm-like trunks.

On giant heather ridges, in wild rolling valleys,
tacazze sunbirds blaze bright
in the soft morning sun.

In golden hypericum, wild dogs mingle, meander,
tease three white-necked ravens,
while buffalo graze.

Still higher, a sole serval, sensing emptiness beginning,
hunts a streaky seed eater
in short tussock grass.

In harsh alpine deserts of gravel and grey scree,
hide striped mice and mole rats
as leopard slinks by.

In rain freezing air drafts, Lammergeier's vast wingspan
wheels over the mountain,
a shadow on rock.

In a strange lunar landscape, stands the crater of Kibo
with her sisters below her –
Mawenzi, Shira.

Climbing up through high cloud to an alien ice world,
where the sun pinks the glaciers,
sculpted by wind.

This is the mountain, freestanding, breathtaking
clouded in mystery,
created in fire.

This is Mount Kilimanjaro

Mount Kilimanjaro stands in the **African Rift Valley** which cuts through East Africa. The valley (6400km long and 50km wide) is dotted with old volcanoes and shallow salt lakes left over from when it formed over a million years ago.

Mount Kilimanjaro in Tanzania is the highest mountain in Africa. The 'White Mountain', as it is generally known, stands alone on the equator, rising from the African plain at just 750m above sea level to 5895m. Climbing Mount Kilimanjaro is like travelling from the Equator to the Arctic Circle through almost every environment on earth, from waterless desert to frozen wastes.

Glaciers are slow-flowing rivers of ice. At one time, an unbroken sheet of ice blanketed the mountain down to 4000m.
Now glaciers are all that remain of the ice and these are slowly disappearing, evaporating into the air instead of melting into rivers. The glaciers, sculpted by wind, are chiselled and fluted into irregular columns and buttresses, hung with slender spines of ice. On the snowfields, irregular spikes of hardened snow resemble hands clasped in prayer.

The summit of Mount Kilimanjaro (5895m) is the crater rim of Kibo, the largest of the three cones. The inner crater rim has hot, smoking fumaroles, deposits of sulphur, water-worn cobbles and frost-shattered boulders. Descending into Kibo's steep inner centre, on a swathe of tiny pea-sized stones is like walking on the moon. At the centre is the great vent.

The inhospitable Alpine desert (4000 – 4900m) is a battle zone for plants. Rocks, boulders, scree and gravel litter the ground. This harsh landscape can be suddenly broken by an eerie 100m-high lava tower. There is little life except tough tussock grass, mosses and lichens and the occasional everlasting flower. It is a cold barren zone of freezing winds and extremes of temperature, where mist soaks the soil and freezes overnight into sharp shards of ice.

In the heath and moorland zone (2800 – 4000m), giant heather forms an enchanted forest bearded with lichen. Ridges and slopes of heather and gorse-like shrub roll and climb into beautiful valleys, heaths and hidden gorges. The slopes are studded with ancient 10m-high giant groundsel, which have cabbage-shaped rosettes of green leaves on the end of naked palm-like trunks. The flowers of giant lobelias, half the height of a giraffe, are sought by iridescent scarlet-tufted Malachite sunbirds and Tacazze, which turn iridescent violet in the sunlight.

A humid rainforest (1800 – 2800m) encircles the mountain. The sun filters down through the dense undergrowth thick with giant ferns. Lianas, lichens and old man's beard festoon the camphor, cedar, juniper, olive, fig, wild mango and tall podocarpus trees. There are many birds such as Hartlaub's Turaco, silvery cheeked hornbills, red-fronted parrots and green pigeons.

The climate in Tanzania consists of two seasons caused by two winds. The south-east trade wind, moist from its passage over the Indian Ocean, brings the long rains between March and May. The north-east monsoon, drier after the longer journey overland, brings the short rains between November and February. A dry period follows the rains. There is a colder season in the middle of the year and a warm one at the end. Because the mountain is on the equator, the higher slopes experience summer every day and winter every night. The lower slopes enjoy on average 2000mm of rain each year, but the summit and crater only have snow, little more than 125mm a year.

Threats to Mount Kilimanjaro

The glaciers on Mount Kilimanjaro are slowly disappearing. This is thought to be partly due to natural causes, but also to global warming. Hundreds of tourists climb the mountain every year, eroding paths, burning fires and leaving rubbish. Illegal hunting, animal poaching, honey gathering, tree felling, collection of wood for fuel, and grass burning are all damaging the mountain's natural environment. The original rainforest has been greatly reduced since 1990 causing loss of cover for animals and the disappearance of a whole host of vital plants. In 1989 the mountain was added to the World Heritage list to protect and maintain the park's natural resources, to control the use of the mountain by local people, and to stop intensive hiking and reduce man-made fires.